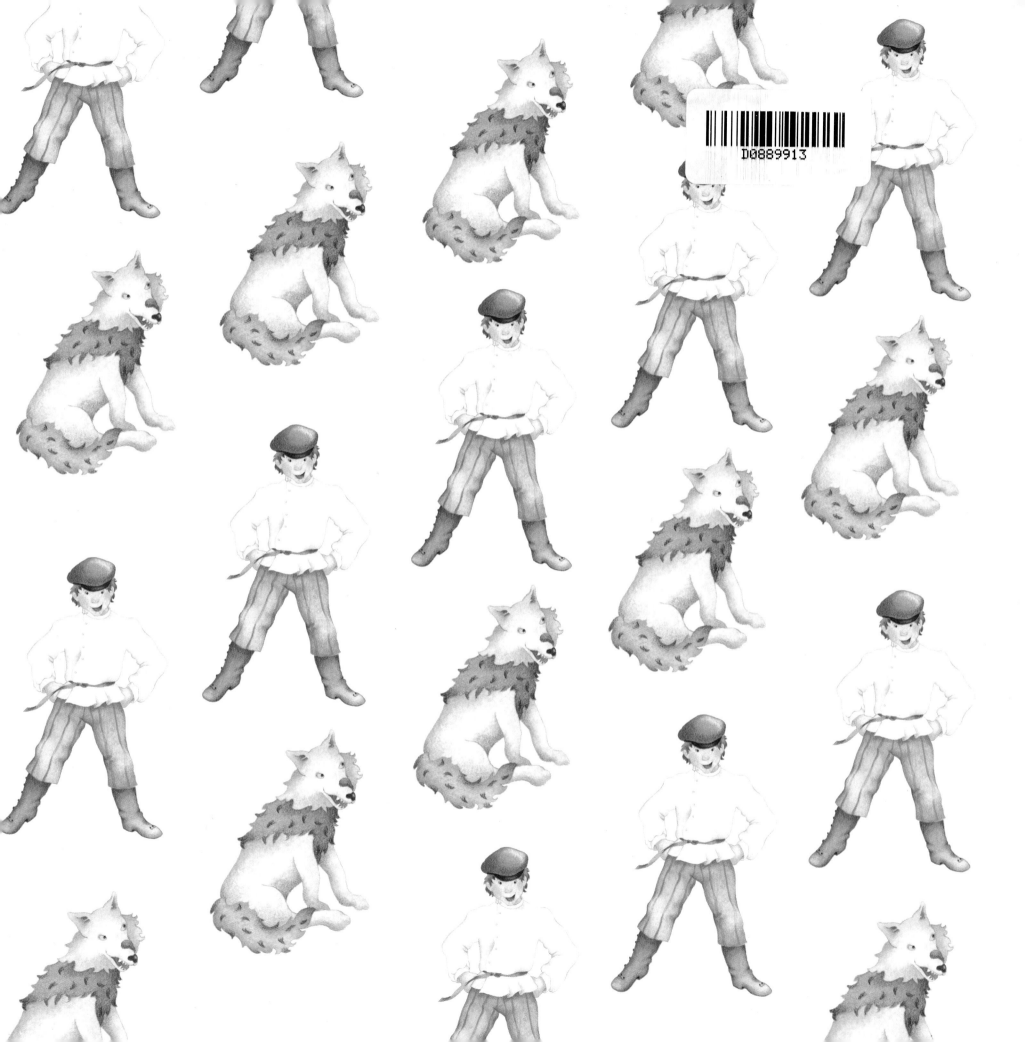

**A FRIEDMAN/FAIRFAX BOOK**

A Life, Times and Music™ Book

© 1997 Michael Friedman Publishing Group.

Library of Congress Cataloging-in-Publication Data

Dewhirst, Carin.

      Peter and the wolf / Carin Dewhirst: illustrations by Naomi Howland.

              p.          cm.

      ISBN 1-56799-540-3 (hardcover)

      1. Prokofiev, Sergey, 1891-1953. Petia i volk.      2. Monologues with music--Stories, plots, etc.--Juvenile literature.

      3. Orchestra--Juvenile literature.      I. Howland, Naomi. II. Title.

ML3930.P77D49  1997

784.2'2--DC21                    97-10154

Editors: Susan Lauzau, Celeste Sollod

Art Director/Designer: Jeff Batzli

Photography Editor: Christopher C. Bain

Illustrator: Naomi Howland

Production Manager: Jeanne E. Hutter

Color separations by HK Scanner Arts Int'l Ltd.

Printed in China by Leefung—Asco Printers Ltd.

10 9 8 7 6 5 4 3 2 1

For bulk purchases and special sales, please contact:

Friedman/Fairfax Publishers

Attention: Sales Department

15 West 26th Street

New York, New York 10010

212/685-6610   FAX 212/685-1307

Visit our website:

http://www.metrobooks.com

## Dedication

*For our beloved early bird, Blake Everett Knutson*

**Photo Credits**

*The Bettman Archive: 22, 23, 24*

*Instrument photographs © Michael Friedman Publishing Group: photographed by Bill Milne*

# CONTENTS

# MEET THE CHARACTERS

There are two ways to meet the characters in Sergei Prokofiev's *Peter and the Wolf*—one way is with words and the other is with music. This clever combination of words and musical notes makes the tale quite endearing. Prokofiev wrote the story and the music as an entertaining way of introducing young children to some of the instruments in an orchestra.

Prokofiev wrote the music in *Peter and the Wolf* for a small orchestra made up of four families, or sections, of instruments. The string section had first and second violins, violas, cellos, and double basses. The wind section had a flute, an oboe, a clarinet, and a bassoon. Prokofiev wrote music for a horn section that included a trumpet, three French horns, and a trombone. Finally, he included parts for various percussion instruments, including kettle drums, triangle, tambourine, cymbals, castanets, snare drum, and bass drum.

There are seven characters in *Peter and the Wolf*, and each one has its own leitmotiv, or melody, played by a different instrument or family of instruments. Have you ever imagined a musical instrument having a personality? As you listen, you might find that you begin to hear each instrument's style or temperament—you will definitely understand why Prokofiev chose a particular instrument for each character. Now it's time to meet the characters and then hear them for yourself.

Peter is a young boy who stays at his grandfather's cottage each summer. Peter loves staying with his grandfather in the country because there are so many places to explore and so many animals to make friends with. He is an imaginative, clever lad who is not afraid of anything. Is Peter too brave for his own good? Read the story and decide for yourself.

Peter is represented by bold string instruments such as the violin or cello. Instruments of the string family come in several sizes. The violin is the smallest and is held under the chin. The viola is a bit larger but is also held under the chin. The cello and double bass are so large that they must rest on pegs on the floor when played. All string instruments make music

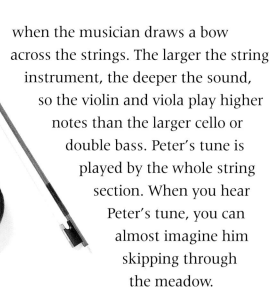

when the musician draws a bow across the strings. The larger the string instrument, the deeper the sound, so the violin and viola play higher notes than the larger cello or double bass. Peter's tune is played by the whole string section. When you hear Peter's tune, you can almost imagine him skipping through the meadow.

Peter's grandfather is rather tired and cranky, but is basically a kind-hearted old man. In his younger days he was quite a prosperous farmer, growing the finest potatoes and beets sold in the markets of neighboring Russian villages. Each year he looks forward to Peter's visits, however, and each year Peter becomes a little bit more adventurous.

The thundering melody for Grandfather is played by a blustering bassoon. Known as a deep wind instrument, the bassoon has a double reed, which is actually two strips of cane or bamboo that vibrate against each other when the musician blows into them. The reed sits at the end of a little metal pipe called a crook. The main body consists of four wooden sections that would measure about eight feet (2½ meters) long if they were laid end to end.

The sound of the bassoon is beautifully deep and rich, giving just a hint of the mellowness or softness in Grandfather's heart.

Peter's day begins when he hears the happy song of a little bluebird sung by a chirping flute. Another member of the group known as wind instruments, a flute is basically a metal tube with holes bored along its length and a mouthpiece at one end. When the player blows across the mouthpiece, the air inside the tube vibrates and creates a sound. You can get the idea by blowing across the mouth of an empty bottle. Different notes are produced by pressing keys, or levers, that cover the holes along the tube. This changes the length of the column of vibrating air—the shorter the column, the higher the tone that is played. The sound of the flute is very much like the lovely song of a bird. The bluebird is one of the best-loved songbirds in the world because of its beautiful colors and its sweet sound.

A plump yellow duck waddles into the story with a quacking tune played by an oboe. Another instrument of the wind family, the oboe—like the bassoon—has a double reed attached to its mouthpiece. Listen and see if you think that the "reedy" sound of an oboe is similar to the quack of a duck.

Peter's cat is represented by a tune played on the clarinet. The clarinet consists of a wooden tube that is very narrow at the top and flared at the bottom. At the top is a single reed, which vibrates against a mouthpiece with a slot in it. The musician creates different tones by using his or her fingers to open or close holes in the wooden tube.

Peter's cat likes to slink around looking for things to pounce upon. If you listen carefully to the cat's tune, you can imagine her sneaking along, carefully placing each velvety paw on the ground. That's because the cat's tune is played a special way on the clarinet. Each note is played in a precise, abrupt way. The musician lets his or her tongue make a definite start and stop to each note—try to say "tut" very quickly and you'll have much the same sort of sound. This technique is called staccato. The music of the clarinet mimics the movements of the cat.

Prokofiev uses three French horns playing together to represent the bold and scary wolf. The French horn has a rich, haunting quality that makes it perfect for portraying the sneaky wolf. The French horn is a very distant relative of the horns used by people during prehistoric times. Thousands of years ago, people made horns out of hollow animal horns, which is how the instrument got its name. The modern French horn is made of a sixteen-foot (5-meter) piece of brass.

Drums are the perfect way to represent the hunters because the banging of a drum is similar to the "bang" of a gun. Drums are part of the percussion section of the orchestra, and all these instruments are played by being hit. Drums, like horns, are very old instruments—we know that they were used in Roman times, at least fifteen hundred years ago. The three hunters are represented by kettle drums and a bass drum. The kettle drum gets its name because it looks like a huge copper kettle. The bass drum is about two or three feet (60 or 90 centimeters) across and has a thicker, looser head, or top. Everyone knows when a bass drum is hit because it's so loud.

# THE TALE OF
# PETER AND THE WOLF

Our story takes place more than a hundred years ago on Peter's grandfather's farm in Russia. Grandfather lives in a cozy cottage surrounded by a cheerful garden. Peter's favorite place to play is the very large tree that has branches which extend over the stone wall that surrounds Grandfather's garden. Near Grandfather's farm is a large, dark forest. Peter has been warned not to play near the forest or even in the inviting meadow that leads to it. Grandfather has always said that the forest holds dangers of all sorts, and Peter is about to find out if he is right or not....

that surrounded the garden, she spied a large animal pacing back and forth, pawing at the ground by the wall. When the animal paused, pointed its nose in the air, and sniffed, Tabby realized that the mysterious animal was a wolf. The cat scurried beneath Peter's bed for safety.

Peter did not know that a very large and hungry wolf had passed by Grandfather's house during the night—but Peter's cat, Tabby, knew. Sometime before dawn she was awakened by something—was it a strange smell or just a noise? She jumped from the bed to the windowsill and peered into the moonlit garden. Just beyond the stone wall

The wolf, meanwhile, paced a while longer until his sharp ears heard footsteps in the distance and his keen nose caught the slightest whiff of gunpowder. Not wanting to run into hunters, the wolf quickly ran off to the nearby forest.

Hunters *were* tracking the wolf. They had followed his tracks from the edge of a nearby village. The hunters tracked the wolf to two farms where he had stolen several chickens and frightened a few farmers. The hunters now stood on the path to Grandfather's house.

They lit their lanterns and began searching for signs of a wolf. A while later one shouted, "Look here!" and the other two hunters rushed to his side. They all lifted their lanterns and looked down the path leading to Grandfather's house. There were the huge, fresh tracks of a full-grown wolf.

The three hunters walked off quickly in the direction of the forest near Grandfather's house. Each man had his gun ready in case he needed to use it.

The sun was beginning to break up the night sky with glowing slivers when Peter first awoke. He yawned and stretched and snuggled deeper into his soft featherbed. The whole world seemed quiet and at rest.

Then, with a flash, Peter remembered that today was the very last day of his visit to Grandfather's house. He had promised himself that it would be the very best day of his entire summer. He shivered with excitement as he tiptoed across the floor and stood at the window.

The view from his upstairs window looked out over Grandfather's splendid garden and over the high stone wall that completely encircled the house. On the other side of the wall stretched a meadow with a clear blue pond nestled in the middle. At the farthest edge of the meadow was the dark, mysterious forest.

Peter sighed. "That meadow is the perfect place to run and play," he thought to himself.

"But Grandfather thinks it's dangerous because it is so close to the forest. He says all sorts of wild and ferocious beasts live there. But I'm not afraid of them!"

As Peter daydreamed, he noticed three hunters walking toward the woods, off on an adventure. He muttered to himself, "Someday, I'm going to march into that dark old forest and catch a wolf all by myself!"

Peter pulled on his striped trousers and buttoned his favorite
shirt. Then he skipped down the path through the flower garden,
opened the large iron gate, and bounded out into the forbidden
meadow, singing to himself:

"Skipping, skipping out the garden gate. Quickly, quickly
before Grandfather awakes. Oh, I wonder what fun
awaits in the meadow past the gate."

"That's the 'skipping-out-the-gate' song,"
Peter thought. "I'll just skip to the
pond and back before Grandfather
even wakes up."

Soon Peter's song was soon joined by another's. It was the twitter-tweet of a bird. Peter heard the familiar chirping tune and smiled as his favorite bluebird fluttered down to say "Good morning."

Soon some quacking notes reached their ears and they turned to see a plump yellow duck waddling toward them from Grandfather's yard. "Wait for me," the duck cried. "I've been dreaming of a dip in that cool, cool pond." In a splash she was in the water.

"Hmmmmmm," thought the bluebird. "That duck is plenty proud and puffed-up."

He flew down and chattered at the duck, "Yoo-hoo, Ducky. How come you're swimming when you could be flying? What kind of a bird are you if you can't fly?"

The duck quacked, "I can fly, but I prefer to swim. What kind of a bird are you if you can't swim?" And with that, the bluebird and the duck held a screeching conversation that kept them both so busy they paid no attention to anyone or anything else.

While the duck and the bluebird continued their
squawking battle along the banks of the pond,
Peter's cat crouched lower and lower, inching
toward the tasty bird as she waited for just
the right moment to POUNCE! "Look out!
Look out!" screamed Peter as the cat
lunged, and the bluebird soared into the
air, landing safe but breathless on the
top of a tree.

"Whew, that was close," sighed
Peter while Tabby circled the tree
trying to decide if she should
climb up after the bird. She soon
realized that by the time she
reached the top, the bird would have flown
away. So instead, she very carefully cleaned
her face and paws and curled up for a
sweet catnap.

All the noise and commotion had awakened Grandfather. He came bellowing out of the house shouting "Peet-tah! Peet-tah!" At last he caught up with his grandson. "Peter, the meadow is not the place to play. How many times do I have to tell you that this place is dangerous! Wolves are hiding in that forest right now, just waiting for someone your size. Suppose a wolf came out of the forest? Then what would you do?" The old man took Peter's hand and led him back inside the high stone wall.

He closed the big iron gate with a bang and locked it up tight.

"I'm sorry, Grandfather," Peter said softly. But deep down inside himself he knew that he had never, not once, not even for one minute…been afraid. What he did not know yet was that Grandfather was almost always right.

Meanwhile, two steely gray eyes were trained on the meadow, focused on the fat yellow duck. As soon as the iron gate clanged shut, the eyes inched forward, peering out as cold as ice from the head of an enormously ferocious wolf. The powerful animal was as swift as he was clever, and only the bird noticed his furtive movements. With a wild and terrified twitter, the bird flew round and round crying warnings. The cat leaped into action. She clawed her way out on a limb of Peter's favorite tree. The bird flitted and fluttered and finally settled on the tip-top of the same tree. The duck waddled as fast as she could toward the safety of Grandfather's garden. But her plump body and wobbly legs were no match for the sleek wolf.

Finally, he was right there behind her, and with one enormous gulp, he swallowed her whole!

Peter had been watching
and listening from his bedroom
window. Now he could see his cat sit-
ting on a branch of the tree at a safe distance from the ground. He could see the bird
perched at the top of the tree on a very thin
branch that could never hold the weight of a cat.
And he was fascinated with the wolf as the animal
paced back and forth alongside the stone wall, his sharp
eyes fixed on the two pairs of eyes in the tree.

Peter ran as quickly and quietly as he could outside and
into the garden. On the ground behind the tree he
found a long, thick piece of rope from a swing that
Grandfather had made for him several summers before. With the rope slung over his shoulder, he
climbed very carefully up into the leafy foliage of the tree until he
was high enough to whisper directions to the bird. "Little bird,
tiny bird, you are the only one who can help me. Fly down and
make the wolf think you are trying to land on his nose. Keep him
busy, but be quick and be careful. That wolf is still hungry!"

17

The bird had not forgotten how, that very morning, Peter had saved his feathered neck from being caught by the cat, and he was delighted to return the favor. He swooped down in a streak and grazed the wolf's nose. The wolf angrily snapped his teeth at the little bird, but the bird's timing was perfect and he missed the sharp teeth and tongue by seconds. The bird flew around and around in larger and larger circles, teasing and tempting the wolf to run and leap and snap at him, but the wolf was always too late.

While the wolf's greedy eyes were focused on the bird, Peter carefully crawled out on the thickest limb of the tree that stretched over the wall. He knotted one end of the rope tightly around the branch and made a large loop at the other end. Slowly, inch by inch, he lowered the loop until it slipped ever so smoothly over the wolf's fluffy tail. Immediately, Peter pulled HARD on his end of the rope and the wolf was caught! The beast squirmed and twisted, but that only pulled the knot tighter as Peter tugged the animal off the ground.

"We've got him, we've got him," cried Peter.
"Together, we've caught the wolf, little bird!"
Just then, several loud shots rang out across
the meadow and the three game hunters
tramped out of the forest with their guns
aimed into the air. "Stop, please," cried Peter.
"Don't shoot! The wolf is already caught!
Look here!"

"Would you help me get this wolf to the zoo?" Peter asked the hunters. "There many people will have a chance to admire him!" The men agreed that Peter had indeed made a fine catch and they tied up the animal securely.

Then Peter organized everyone into a line, and they all marched in one grand procession to the zoo. Leading the parade was Peter with the little bird proudly perched on the brim of his hat. Then came the hunters pulling the wolf. Even the duck could be heard swimming around inside the wolf, since the wolf had swallowed her whole. Grandfather brought up the rear, carrying the cat and muttering, "What if Peter hadn't caught the wolf? What if there had been two wolves? What then? That would have been... " But Peter, of course, was grinning from one ear to the other and back again. He had actually caught a wolf, and this last day with Grandfather really did turn out to be the best one of all.

# ABOUT THE COMPOSER

Before Sergei Prokofiev wrote *Peter and the Wolf*, he had spent more than twenty years composing music. He was born in 1891 in an area now known as Dnepropetrovsk in the Ukraine. Prokofiev's mother was an accomplished pianist and from her he learned the basics of music at a young age. At age thirteen Prokofiev enrolled in the conservatory at St. Petersburg, where he was taught by many famous composers and musicians, including Nikolai Rimsky-Korsakov and Anatol Liadov.

As a young man Prokofiev showed great talent for composing music, and his early works were considered quite modern and even daring. One of his most famous pieces, called *Classical Symphony*, was written almost eighty years ago and helped set musical trends that have lasted throughout the twentieth century.

In 1919 Prokofiev traveled to the United States and Europe to conduct and give piano concerts, and while he was abroad he wrote ballets, operas, and symphonies. He settled in Paris and lived there for more than ten years, continuing to write music, including two ballets for his friend Sergei Diaghilev, head of the Ballet Russes. Prokofiev later moved back to the Soviet Union, and it was in his homeland that he wrote *Peter and the Wolf*, his best-known work. He also continued to write ballets, operas, and other compositions, many of them in tribute to

the Soviet state, and he even contributed the scores to several films.

In 1953, at the age of sixty-one, he died in Moscow where his last major work, a ballet called *A Tale of the Stone Flower*, was in production.

## ABOUT THE CONDUCTOR AND NARRATOR

Many people, including Sergei Prokofiev's daughter, have recorded the narration for *Peter and the Wolf*. The voice you hear on this CD is that of Leonard Bernstein, a famous conductor, composer, pianist, and author. Bernstein is the perfect person to narrate *Peter and the Wolf* because just like Sergei Prokofiev, Bernstein wanted to help children appreciate music.

Leonard Bernstein was born in Lawrence, Massachusetts, in 1918, and as a child he loved music. When he was young, Bernstein's Aunt Clara gave his family an upright piano. He was ten years old when the piano arrived and he immediately began imitating songs he heard on the radio. He began taking formal piano lessons from a young woman who lived nearby. By the time he was thirteen he could play more difficult pieces than his teacher could. She told Bernstein's mother that he was gifted and suggested that a professional teacher from the New England Conservatory of Music in Boston be found for him.

Bernstein's father did not want to pay for expensive lessons, so Bernstein himself taught piano lessons to the local children. In addition, he played the piano with a jazz band that entertained guests at weddings and other events on the weekend.

Although Bernstein's father was not pleased that his son wanted to be a musician, he became more supportive. He bought his son a grand piano and took him to classical music concerts. Bernstein continued to develop his talent as a pianist, and at age fifteen he also began putting on elaborate operas during the summer. Bernstein organized it all—the dancing, music, and costumes—and the shows were a success. His first show was a comic version of the opera

*Carmen*, and for the show the boys played girls' parts and the girls took the boys' roles. It was a very silly piece, but this was just the start, for Bernstein would continue putting on theatrical shows for his entire career.

After attending Boston Latin School, Bernstein went to Harvard University and the Curtis Institute of Music. He then moved to New York City and was appointed assistant conductor of the New York Philharmonic. On November 14, 1943, the head conductor got sick and Bernstein had to take his place. Bernstein was very nervous because he had never conducted many of the pieces the orchestra was going to play. In addition, the concert was going to be broadcast from Carnegie Hall on the radio as a live performance, so any mistakes would be heard by thousands of listeners. The concert was a great success and afterward Bernstein received many offers to conduct.

Bernstein became musical director of the New York City Symphony several years after his brilliant debut with the Philharmonic. During the next fifteen years he taught, conducted, and composed music. One of Bernstein's most popular compositions was a musical called *West Side Story*, which was a retelling of William Shakespeare's play *Romeo and Juliet*. The musical was a hit and was later made into a movie. In 1957 he became musical director of the New York Philharmonic. He was very popular as a conductor, and when he retired in 1969, he was made an honorary conductor for life.

By the time Bernstein became musical director of the Philharmonic, he had a family and was eager to teach his two children, Jamie and Alexander, about music. Although Bernstein did not write music for children as Prokofiev had, he hosted and conducted a television series called *Young People's Concerts*. Bernstein's shows were taped live, first at Carnegie Hall and then in Philharmonic Hall in New York City. They were so popular that there was a waiting list of two thousand children to see a live perfomance—some parents put their children on the list the day their kids were born!

Leonard Bernstein made music his life. As a conductor and a composer he was known for his passion and so, perhaps, he also brought new life to music. After a long and brilliant career, Bernstein died in New York in 1990 at the age of seventy-two.